Rookie reader®

Messy Bessey's
Garden

Written by Patricia and Fredrick McKissack
Illustrated by Dana Regan

Children's Press®
A Division of Scholastic Inc.
New York • Toronto • London • Auckland • Sydney
Mexico City • New Delhi • Hong Kong
Danbury, Connecticut

For Sarilda Blake, to share with Michelle
—P. and F.M.

To Joe and Tommy, who grow the best
Halloween pumpkins in town
—D.R.

Reading Consultants
Linda Cornwell
Literacy Specialist

Katharine A. Kane
Education Consultant
(Retired, San Diego County Office of Education
and San Diego State University)

Library of Congress Cataloging-in-Publication Data

McKissack, Pat, 1944-
    Messy Bessey's garden / written by Patricia and Fredrick McKissack ;
illustrated by Dana Regan.
        p. cm. —(Rookie reader)
    Summary: Messy Bessey discovers that with proper care her garden will
flourish.
    ISBN 0-516-22491-3 (lib. bdg.)   0-516-27386-8 (pbk.)
    [1. Gardening—Fiction. 2. African Americans—Fiction. 3. Stories in rhyme.]
I. McKissack, Fredrick. II. Regan, Dana, ill. III. Title. IV. Series.
    PZ8. 3. M224 Mdp 2002
    [E]—dc21

                        2001047203

CHILDREN'S PRESS, and A ROOKIE READER®, and associated logos are trademarks
and or registered trademarks of Scholastic Library Publishing. SCHOLASTIC and
associated logos are trademarks and or registered trademarks of Scholastic Inc.

   6 7 8 9 10 11 12 13 14 R 14 13 12 11 10 09 08 07 06

It's spring again, Miss Bessey.
No more ice and snow.

3

Come. It's time to plant your seeds and watch your garden grow.

Dig a hole.

Put in a seed.

Plant them row by row.

Cover them up.
Water them well.

Now, let the garden grow.

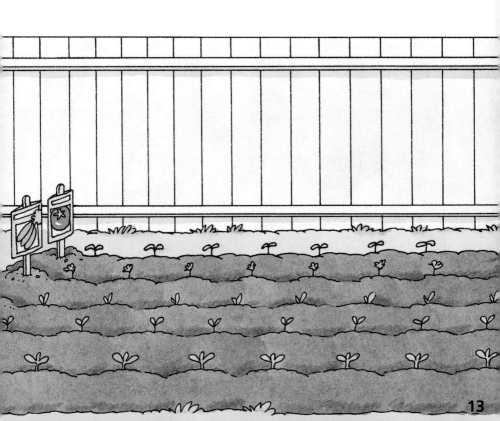

14

No, no, no, Messy Bessey!
Plants need help to grow.

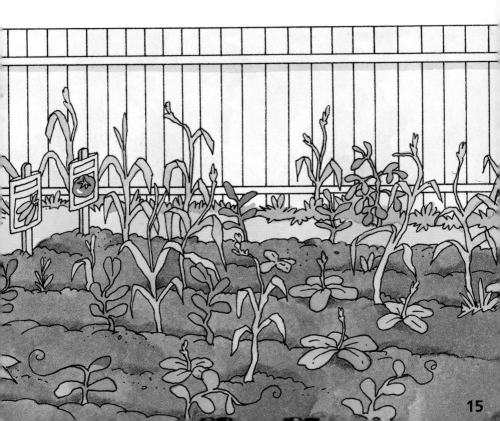

You haven't taken care of them.
You've let your garden go.

So get the shovel.
Get the hoe.

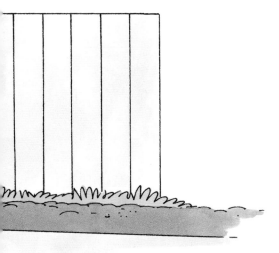

Water every row.

Pull the weeds.

Snip and cut.

Help your garden grow.

Fall has come at last, Miss Bess.

Now, don't you feel just fine?
Your garden is a big success . . .

with pumpkins on the vine!

Word List (71 words)

a	garden	more	spring
again	get	need	success
and	go	no	taken
at	grow	now	the
Bess	has	of	them
Bessey	haven't	on	time
big	help	plant	to
by	hoe	plants	up
care	hole	pull	vine
come	ice	pumpkins	watch
cover	in	put	water
cut	is	row	weeds
dig	it's	seed	well
don't	just	seeds	with
every	last	shovel	you
fall	let	snip	your
feel	messy	snow	you've
fine	Miss	so	

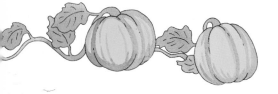 

About the Authors

Patricia and Fredrick McKissack are freelance writers and editors, living in St. Louis County, Missouri. Their awards as authors include the Coretta Scott King Award, the Jane Addams Peace Award, the Newbery Honor, and the 1998 Regina Medal from the Catholic Library Association. The McKissacks have also written many other *Messy Bessey* books in the Rookie Reader series.

About the Illustrator

Dana Regan lives in Kansas City, Missouri, with her sons, Joe and Tommy, who are very good gardeners, especially when it is time to water things with the garden hose.